To :  ford

12/2/2003

The Countries of the United Nations
Name Poems of the 191 Member States

is dedicated to
all the people of the world.

*Thank you to the following people
who helped to make this publication possible:*
Francesco Dae Sun Kim
Ju Bong Kil
John Heinz
David Mericnyak
Kevin Daly and Stephanie Daly
Andrew Liao
Michael Pierce
John Avault and Andrew Avault
Christopher Malloy
John White, III
Thomas Kuklinski
Nancy Lam
Mario Amelio
Marco Visioli
Domenico Miceli
Luigia Tarantino
Antonella Tarantino
Giordano Difiore
Marco Monaldi
Peter Ryan
Stephanie Kenney
Ryan Kirkby, in Memory of Patricia Kirkby
Margaret Codianni
Gregory and Kathryn Chadbourne
Patricia Morey
Thomas Healy
Michael Ralph
Timothy Rutherford
Alex Cardona
Jonathan Bradley Schell

A very special thank you to:
Kathryn Adah Stackhouse

The Countries of the United Nations

Name Poems of the 191 Member States

By

World Shim Gum Do Founding Master
Zen Master Chang Sik Kim

Edited by
World Shim Gum Do Head Master
Mary Jeanette Stackhouse Kim

The Countries of the United Nations
Name Poems of the 191 Member States
Copyright © 2003 by Zen Master Chang Sik Kim

All rights reserved. No part of this book may be
reproduced, stored in a retrieval system,
or transmitted in any form or by any means,
electronic, mechanical, photocopying, recording or
otherwise, without permission.

ISBN 0-9676479-5-9

Published by

World Shim Gum Do Association, Inc.
203 Chestnut Hill Avenue
Brighton, Massachusetts 02135
United States of American
www.shimgumdo.org

Library of Congress Control Number:
2003114064

Other Books by
World Shim Gum Do Founding Master
Zen Master Chang Sik Kim

The Art of Zen Sword
The History of Shim Gum Do

The Pillowhead Collects Your Dreams

Happy Birthday To You
Birthday Poems, Name Poems,
Marriage Poems and Memorials

The Sky Is Blue The Water Is Clear

The Stars Shine The Ocean Is Blue

The World's Flowers

The Wind Never Stops

The Wind Never Stops . . . will reach new audiences of both poets and Zen believers with a hard-hitting set of works which are diverse. They tell stories, they paint pictures, and they provide beautiful powerful insights which invite re-reading. . . . Outstanding.

Library Bookwatch, The Midwest Book Review

The images of the Western Hemisphere on the front cover and the Eastern Hemisphere on the back cover are courtesy of NASA.

Credits:
NASA Goddard Space Flight Center
Image by Reto Stöckli
Enhancements by Robert Simmon

Foreword

The poems contained in this volume are about the 191 United Nations Member States. After deep contemplation, Zen Master Chang Sik Kim wrote these poems from his heart in just four days, from March 3rd through March 6th, 2003. It is his wish to portray the universal goodness of all people. As humanity moves forward, our world is filled with great potential, yet there is much uncertainty. In writing of the goodness and the greatness of the people and their countries, it is Zen Master Kim's wish that good fortune will follow for our world. With good will, all human beings can experience the power of love and compassion, and world peace can be attained.

The countries written about in the poems contained in this volume are those that are current Member States of the United Nations. The names of the countries appear in this volume in the order presented on the United Nations list of Member States. No offense or disrespect is intended in the use of what may be considered a short or more common name. The essence of these poems is for all the people of the world regardless of their race, national origin, or religion; and the message is that of peace.

World Shim Gum Do Founding Master
Zen Master Chang Sik Kim

World Shim Gum Do Head Master
Mary Jeanette Stackhouse Kim
Editor

The Countries of the United Nations
Name Poems of the 191 Member States

Afghanistan	1
Albania	2
Algeria	3
Andorra	4
Angola	5
Antigua and Barbuda	6
Argentina	7
Armenia	8
Australia	9
Austria	10
Azerbaijan	11
Bahamas	12
Bahrain	13
Bangladesh	14
Barbados	15
Belarus	16
Belgium	17
Belize	18
Benin	19
Bhutan	20
Bolivia	21
Bosnia and Herzegovina	22
Botswana	23
Brazil	24
Brunei Darussalam	25
Bulgaria	26
Burkina Faso	27
Burundi	28
Cambodia	29
Cameroon	30

Canada 31
Cape Verde 32
Central African Republic 33
Chad 34
Chile 35
China 36
Columbia 37
Comoros 38
Congo 39
Costa Rica 40
Côte d'Ivoire 41
Croatia 42
Cuba 43
Cyprus 44
Czech Republic 45
Democratic People's Republic of Korea 46
Democratic Republic of the Congo 47
Denmark 48
Djibouti 49
Dominica 50
Dominican Republic 51
Ecuador 52
Egypt 53
El Salvador 54
Equatorial Guinea 55
Eritrea 56
Estonia 57
Ethiopia 58
Fiji 59
Finland 60
France 61
Gabon 62
Gambia 63
Georgia 64
Germany 65

Ghana	66
Greece	67
Grenada	68
Guatemala	69
Guinea	70
Guinea-Bissau	71
Guyana	72
Haiti	73
Honduras	74
Hungary	75
Iceland	76
India	77
Indonesia	78
Iran	79
Iraq	80
Ireland	81
Israel	82
Italy	83
Jamaica	84
Japan	85
Jordan	86
Kazakhstan	87
Kenya	88
Kiribati	89
Kuwait	90
Kyrgyzstan	91
Lao People's Democratic Republic	92
Latvia	93
Lebanon	94
Lesotho	95
Liberia	96
Libyan Arab Jamahiriya	97
Liechtenstein	98
Lithuania	99
Luxembourg	100

Madagascar	101
Malawi	102
Malaysia	103
Maldives	104
Mali	105
Malta	106
Marshall Islands	107
Mauritania	108
Mauritius	109
Mexico	110
Micronesia	111
Monaco	112
Mongolia	113
Morocco	114
Mozambique	115
Myanmar	116
Namibia	117
Nauru	118
Nepal	119
Netherlands	120
New Zealand	121
Nicaragua	122
Niger	123
Nigeria	124
Norway	125
Oman	126
Pakistan	127
Palau	128
Panama	129
Papua New Guinea	130
Paraguay	131
Peru	132
Philippines	133
Poland	134
Portugal	135

Qatar	136
Republic of Korea	137
Republic of Moldova	138
Romania	139
Russian Federation	140
Rwanda	141
Saint Kitts and Nevis	142
Saint Lucia	143
Saint Vincent and the Grenadines	144
Samoa	145
San Marino	146
Sao Tome and Principe	147
Saudi Arabia	148
Senegal	149
Serbia and Montenegro	150
Seychelles	151
Sierra Leone	152
Singapore	153
Slovakia	154
Slovenia	155
Solomon Islands	156
Somalia	157
South Africa	158
Spain	159
Sri Lanka	160
Sudan	161
Suriname	162
Swaziland	163
Sweden	164
Switzerland	165
Syrian Arab Republic	166
Tajikistan	167
Thailand	168
The former Yugoslav Republic of Macedonia	169
Timor-Leste	170

Togo	171
Tonga	172
Trinidad and Tobago	173
Tunisia	174
Turkey	175
Turkmenistan	176
Tuvalu	177
Uganda	178
Ukraine	179
United Arab Emirates	180
United Kingdom of Great Britain and Northern Ireland	181
United Republic of Tanzania	182
United States of America	183
Uruguay	184
Uzbekistan	185
Vanuatu	186
Venezuela	187
Viet Nam	188
Yemen	189
Zambia	190
Zimbabwe	191
The Universe	192
The Stars	194
Earth	195
The United Nations	196
About Zen Master Chang Sik Kim	198

The Countries of the United Nations

Name Poems of the 191 Member States

By

World Shim Gum Do Founding Master
Zen Master Chang Sik Kim

Edited by
World Shim Gum Do Head Master
Mary Jeanette Stackhouse Kim

Afghanistan

Early in the morning, the bright light of Sir Sun's
    eyes arrives on the tallest mountain.
All kinds of news goes everywhere
    and shakes the whole world.
People keep going, the mountain never ends.
The dream's breathing is just like life.
Each person appears, they try to work hard,
The snow mountain dances in front of them.
The land is strong,
Life is great,
It makes the sky breathe blue.

Albania

Inside the egg, there are the sounds of dreaming.
The great truth appears.
In each book, on each page, vital history wakes up.
You cannot keep any secrets,
> as moment by moment,
> everything is announced.

Nobody can copy your heart,
That is your country's treasure.

Algeria

Try to understand,
    That is wisdom.
In wisdom, the truth is dancing.
The strongest person cannot pick up
    and throw the sky and earth.
You cannot argue about it,
    That is beautiful;
That makes every neighborhood happy.
Early in the morning and late in the afternoon,
    Sir Sun has the same face;
That is truth,
It never changes.

Andorra

Inside is enjoyment,
Love and compassion make the dream bigger.
Nobody can block the flowing water.
Ra, ra, ra is inside the rhythm,
The faces of all the people understand each other.

Angola

Angola, Angola,
Your great heart is beautiful,
It shows its greatness.
Continue,
for trillions and trillions of years,
keep going.
That is wisdom.
Wisdom never calculates.

Antigua and Barbuda

The mind is peaceful, the thoughts are clear.
The past, present and future are dancing.
Antigua and Barbuda create gold,
      and it appears everywhere.
The feet of the people are not lazy,
Everything wakes up.
The dream tries to be reborn again.
The dream makes the blue sky dance.

Argentina

The mind tries to understand;
Thinking carries a lamp.
Your action is always measured.
Beauty doesn't have any dust.
You and I always work hard,
That gives life to the tape measure,
      again.

Armenia

The news is announced,
It goes to everybody's heart
 and makes their flower open.
If you cut through attachment,
At that point, your original root appears.
My mind and your mind come together.
Our thoughts make a flower that hits the sky.
The beautiful treasure looks for who works hard.

Australia

People come and go,
Their heart's great dream opens the road.
Everybody appears and works hard,
The rivers and mountains present them
      with their essence.
You make your memory clear,
Inside your history everybody holds the book,
That book is very thick.
The train runs on the rail,
The train's dreaming pushes today and tomorrow.
The truth holds onto one flower,
      looking for who can understand.
Look at yourself, you don't have any mistakes,
That is truly beautiful.

Austria

Today announces tomorrow,
Tomorrow's dream pushes the future.
The road is very smooth.
Sir Lover comes and goes,
The road does not make any gate.
Summer's truth wakes up dreaming.
In the Fall, all the grain is collected.
One song makes the mountains, the plains,
    and the blue sky clear.

Azerbaijan

The roller skater's speed makes the heart nervous.
On the small road and the big road,
    the roller skater is busy.
The mind cannot measure,
Thinking always calculates.
Nobody can help you,
You stand up by yourself.
Your consciousness is clear,
The pine tree can understand that.
From hard work, sweat appears and holds onto
    the forehead.
The fortune is dancing.
The water and wind are so quiet,
They announce who you are.

Bahamas

On the stone, the blue sky invites the Stars.
All day long, in the sky,
      Sir Sun dreams in his heart.
Sir Sun's heart introduces who you are.
The mind is great,
Thinking and action stand up and open their eyes.
Clear love and compassion open today
      and tomorrow.

Bahrain

The walking footsteps push today away;
The walking footprints invite tomorrow.
People's lives are never free.
Everyone's wants are counted clearly.
The highest and most beautiful fortune
    is in front of you,
The mountains and rivers dance.

Bangladesh

In the room, the whole family sits together
    and helps each other,
That makes history wake up.
Every moment the forest becomes clear,
It breathes in and out,
That sound makes the mountain wake up again.
The grass and trees all line up,
The words of the great Dharma appear,
    no one can open their mouths.
The grass and trees can read them.
The birds always try a new location,
They sing to each other, they love each other.
Keep going, never stop,
Everything wakes up,
Show them the correct way.

Barbados

History grows up and makes every Barbadian
    work hard.
When you lie down,
    the pillow announces the night world,
    the sky and the earth.
Your knowledge never uses a measure,
but you understand the correct measurement.
On the side of the road, the flower dances,
It pinches the highest perfume point.
Sitting down or standing up,
    your thinking can see
    where the measurement ends.

Belarus

You try to harvest the grain with a sickle,
The faces of the grain show you
    what new life is about.
In the bowl, the noodles proclaim philosophy.
The stomach has strong energy,
The other organs' eyes are very sensitive.
The happiness in the house talks
    about the sky and earth.
The wind follows the water,
The wind makes all the rivers and oceans wake up.

Belgium

The bell sound wakes time up.
The day is bright,
It opens everyday and makes everything grow.
After lunch, the mind is peaceful.
Love grows,
The truth flower appears,
Every thought hangs from that flower.

Belize

The roots of the grass and trees wake up the root
    of the Universal and it dreams.
Loss and prosperity are controlled by calculations.
The night's great energy creates new dreaming
    that opens tomorrow brightly.

Benin

Weaving makes fabric;
The fabric announces
     what love and compassion are to everybody.
The cooking pot understands how to boil water.
The truth of everything in the Universe
     is in the pot,
It cannot leave.

Bhutan

Hard work is the greatest life,
It touches the human heart.
On the strongest road, the wind and the clouds
    hold onto their hearts, very carefully;
They learn about the truth.

Bolivia

Look into the mind;
The mirror holds thinking, and dances,
The mind, the mirror, and thinking
      make tomorrow wake up.
They introduce each other.
The rain drops carries the truth.
They are spread out over the mountains and rivers,
The rain drops make the flowers appear.

Bosnia and Herzegovina

The four seasons chase each other.
The end of each season relays itself to the next,
They never argue about ownership,
They only keep compassion.
The beautiful valley appears and is enjoyed
      by the perfume of the trees and grass.
Their love is very rich,
They are very handsome.
The four seasons always connect
      to the grass and trees,
They never argue about what is worthless,
Their faces are so beautiful.
Archeologists carry their notebooks and pens
      and visit the valley.
Whether the rain comes or not,
The blue sky can understand the cloud's true mind.
The guest visits for a short time
      and learns about compassion,
They are awakened for their lifetime.

Botswana

You knock on doors, day and night,
Looking for the face of the one you want.
From the first time the face is met,
    you are friends for life.
That makes a truth flower.
The wine touches the heart,
That feeling is rich.
The body wakes up,
Its balance is alive.
The bell sound introduces you and me,
That makes the sky and earth great.

Brazil

You look great.
Your heart holds a flower,
You look to the biggest mountain,
Its heart opens and runs to visit you.
You cannot understand each other;
You and the mountain have a feeling,
That feeling makes the truth come through,
That wakes up the seasons.
The stream water and river water flow,
Carrying the faces of the grass and trees.
When the flowing water meets the ocean,
It changes the ocean's face to grass and trees.

Brunei Darussalam

If there is not enough,
      the people share with each other.
The ruby never brags about its color,
The ruby's big heart never counts how old it is;
      That is beautiful.
The neighborhood carries on, just like a family.
Sir Moon visits, softly,
Sir Moon loses his own dreaming.
In each house, Sir Moon's dreaming has life.
Everybody is compassionate to each other,
That fills the well with water.
Whoever is thirsty is given life again.

Bulgaria

Call Sir Lover.
The wind opens its ears and runs in,
The wind washes its mouth in the water.
Every family makes happiness,
They work hard.
The calculator counts,
Day and night meet each other,
The grass and trees understand,
They dance.
The birds understand,
They fly into the sky.
In the morning, afternoon and night,
The flowers open.
The perfume hits the bell,
The bell sound introduces the sky and earth.

Burkina Faso

The black hole swallows the Universe.
The darkness of the night learns from the black hole.
The night makes everybody sleep,
They dream.
The dreaming makes strong energy,
That makes the sky and earth clear,
That energy make the country appear clearly,
The day and night fall to their knees.
Everyone's lives have thousands
       and millions of experiences,
They hit history's bell.
Wherever that news goes, it makes a well.
The well dances excellently.

Burundi

The village is built, block by block,
The village picks up yesterday's compassion,
 and builds the compassion of today.
The compassion of today makes future love.
The eye never measures,
That is wisdom.
The wisdom is as high as the stars,
The stars cover the Universe.
The foundation of great energy
 announces future history.

Cambodia

The night is very dark,
The stars are very shiny,
The stars carry their dreams and visit the people.
The stars present their dreaming
      to the people's hearts.
Everybody throws away gossip, and what they
      don't understand about each other.
Clarity appears and shows the original root.
The shadow in each footprint cannot lie.
Early in the morning Sir Sun arrives,
His eye's light cleans everything out.

Cameroon

The camera lens opens and closes,
It carries thinking;
Thinking cannot throw the mind away.
Cameroon points,
On that point,
      the sky and earth try to open the flower,
The sky and earth chase the day and night.

Canada

A strong voice hits the earth and sky,
The earth and sky wake up.
The mountains, rivers, grass and trees look
 at you and me, and everybody,
That is beautiful.
That beauty goes to every sidewalk,
Every neighborhood is clear,
Their love and compassion fill the sidewalks.

Cape Verde

Dig deep into the ground,
Inside, the seeds open their eyes.
The sounds of the lives are beautiful,
The seeds' action appears on the ground,
        beautifully.
The seeds' perfume flies around the grass and trees,
The butterflies and bees dance
        around the neighborhood.
The neighborhood comes together,
The people's hearts flow beautifully.

Central African Republic

The wind moves sensationally,
It collects the mountains and plains.
The first meeting time of two people
    makes their thinking clear.
The rain falls like a sauna,
The sound of the raindrops hitting the ground
    is like the sound of clapping hands.
Africa keeps dreaming strongly,
That energy goes everywhere.
Wisdom can understand action,
Wisdom is put on the highest mountain,
Wisdom talks about the blue sky
    and about what is never ending.

Chad

You carry the biggest sword.
You swing the sword one time,
That makes the mountains and plains clear.
Every face appears,
Wisdom is drawn on each face.
They take care of the neighborhood,
       just as though it was their own house.

Chile

Paint appears everywhere beautifully,
    just like a flower.
You look, and look again,
The paint always looks brand new.
You understand that keeping
    tomorrow's appointment is very important.
The friendship goes 10,000,000 years,
    continuously.

China

Everybody's heart is filled with dreams.
The dreaming announces tomorrow.
Everybody's concentration makes
    one mind appear.
The soft voice sounds humble,
The humble sounds become a tape measure,
The tape measure tells the sky and earth
    what to do.

Columbia

In front of you,
> the sweet cola taste cannot move.

You look so great,
You announce what human life is.
The rain's news makes all of nature prosper,
Nobody knows the mind mirror.
The mirror shows the sky and earth.

Comoros

You have a dialogue with the tallest mountain,
The wind listens,
The wind's ears open,
The wind makes love and compassion
      come together inside everyone's hearts.
Your action is soft,
You announce the truth.
Everybody prays and works hard.
The dirt is happy,
The sky is content.

Congo

You make strong sounds.
The truth is shocked,
The truth opens its ears and runs into you.
The Geologists open their eyes,
They carry their pens and notebooks,
They check the mountains and rivers.
Congo is great,
The greatness never counts the seasons.

Costa Rica

The mountains, rivers, plants, animals,
     and human beings grow faces
     and put them in their own minds.
They make their own thinking,
Their thinking makes their bodies clear.
They never point and never argue
     about each other,
That is wisdom.
Action appears clearly,
Nobody argues,
The voice is so clear,
They take care of each other.

Côte d'Ivoire

Inside, the nose smells the mother's fragrance.
The blue sky opens,
The blue sky looks for a stone to stand on.
The beautiful watch the blue sky,
The beautiful look at the eggs and the seeds;
They open and create the sky and earth.

Croatia

The seasons' dreaming is put into the clover leaves.
Every road is filled with perfume.
The mind is romantic.
You remember what you forgot.
The camera takes a shot,
Capturing the past, present, and future
Their eyes appear, point by point
      on the piece of paper.

Cuba

Ready, go!
Actresses and Actors act,
Nature constantly moves,
following its own scenario.
Everyone's hands grab something.
The mirror's face is so clear.
The mirror looks for who wants something.

Cyprus

The bag is filled with love and compassion.
Early in the morning, Sir Sun brings a bright bag,
It wakes up the rivers and mountains.
The grass roots clean the water.
The lamp makes every year bright.
Your mind becomes clear and bright.
It opens today and tomorrow.

Czech Republic

Inside the body, moment by moment,
      the organs never stop.
The body grows bigger,
      It grabs the dirt and the sky.
Wisdom's seeds have a strong direction.
Everybody who understands runs into that point.
The finger points to the blue sky,
      That measures the strength of wisdom.

North Korea

The lamp is in front of your nose.
Inside the light, the universe is dancing.
Your consciousness is very strong,
It hits the earth and cuts through the sky.
You understand or you don't understand,
It doesn't matter,
Your country's name is famous,
The name is Sham Chun Lee Gum Su Gang San.

'Sham Chun Lee' means: 1200 Kilometers
'Gum Su Gang San' means: Gold Land and Mountains

Democratic Republic of the Congo

Boiling water creates food,
That food helps healthiness
    to appear in the people,
The family grows bigger.
The compass points to the tallest mountain,
The mountain becomes hot.
The tallest mountain never questions the compass.
The tallest mountain looks great,
The tallest mountain announces its meaning,
Congo holds the biggest mind.

Denmark

Dancing is the supreme enjoyment
      in the sky and earth.
The grass and trees learn how to dance
      from the four seasons.
With one word, the poet makes the sky and earth
      turn over,
That shocks the bookstore.
The biggest hands create the mountains and rivers.

Djibouti

The highest wisdom shows what the mind is.
Hard work wakes everything up.
Such clear thinking scares the universe.

Dominica

Great energy makes knowledge see its own roots.
Natural energy takes care of everything,
    It doesn't ask for wages.
The beautiful song makes the ears happy.
The beauty of Dominica shocks the world.

Dominican Republic

The helping hand is beautiful.
Don't be attached to anything.
Clear consciousness fills every room.
Clear thinking never argues with anything,
Clear thinking goes to the whole world.
The people of the world understand you,
They bring their own bigger mind.

Ecuador

In the egg, the life dreams of the sky and earth.
The food on the fork shows what is great,
    what is true and what is beautiful.
The fork opens wisdom's life.
If anything challenges you,
    your consciousness is strong;
You never give up.
The nations of nature line up,
Beautiful dreaming appears on their faces.

Egypt

The sand makes all the neighborhoods.
Each grain of sand holds onto the golden light.
The seasons run into the sand,
They cannot do anything.
Each house displays a pure flag,
The flags collect all the wind.
The sky opens blue and collects the star flowers.
The star flowers plant golden light
      in each grain of sand.

El Salvador

Everybody's name is in the telephone directory.
Each name is beautiful.
Thinking is life,
The roots of thinking keep the mind mirror.
The road goes straight, it never ends.
The stars line up on the side of the road.
The stars' faces never brag about themselves.
That is the biggest truth.

Equatorial Guinea

In the mind, the memory box makes a flower.
The perfume mirror goes to everybody.
They know each other,
That opens love and compassion.
The neighborhood is contained inside one wall.

Eritrea

Thinking points everywhere,
The mind holds onto the mirror.
The wind follows the rhythm,
The wind invites the clouds.
The dancing clouds make raindrops,
The rain feeds the roots of all life.
The memory looks for and finds its motherland.
The happy news comes from 1,000 miles away,
The news makes happiness from morning to night.

Estonia

Fixing the problem and taking good care of it,
      is the fortune of the sky and earth.
Your concentration stands straight up,
Nobody knew about that.
Originally, love and compassion
      were made from dirt.
You and I shake hands,
The blue sky counts that,
The mountains and rivers don't understand,
The blue sky teaches them.

Ethiopia

Wisdom understands how to lose and how to win.
In the sky and earth, that is great.
The wind never blocks out that point,
The wind makes the clouds and dirt wealthy.
The morning and afternoon
      never made their names,
The day only keeps going.
The flower understands morning and evening,
The perfume tastes everything
      and the names appear.
Your country is not missing,
Your country's philosophy is its treasure.

Fiji

The new faces appear,
They make history continue.
They plant everything,
The bigger mind never barricades the villages.
The four seasons look for the bigger mind,
They push every day.

Finland

The flower bud invites Spring.
Spring opens the flower.
The flower counts the four seasons,
It keeps one point.
The lens doesn't lie,
It opens its eye once and it never closes it.
Finland's energy is great.
The energy powerfully pushes the four seasons,
They tumble and tumble.

France

The grain grows,
It is a healthy green;
That shows that truth is great and beautiful.
The truth is with the grain,
The truth shows every season to everybody,
The seasons make the people clear.
They provide shelter for those in need,
They bury compassion in their hearts.
Life is healthy,
Your country is completely filled
    with its philosophy of life.

Gabon

The families and cities of Gabon are its treasure.
They help each other,
That is great energy.
One flower announces that.
The original motherland is the root of the Universe.
The root's fragrance is beautiful.
The beautiful talk about the never-changing truth.

Gambia

The mind is thankful,
Thinking is clear,
Action is beautiful.
That brings life to today and tomorrow.
The rain comes through the mountains and rivers.
The well holds the mirror,
It learns about philosophy.
Low and high, the truth is the same.
The wind and clouds announce that point.

Georgia

The stream water flows and makes a river,
The ocean appears.
The ocean's blue color looks for that
    which is above the blue sky.
Wisdom's measure knocks on the sky and earth
    and makes the Universe wake up.
The Universe shows off its magnitude.

Germany

Prostrates can understand the great truth.
Everybody helps each other,
They question about the truth.
Moment by moment, thinking is very sharp,
That opens the mind,
The mind shows the mirror.
Clean out the nicotine,
       and the original point appears clearly.

Ghana

The mind keeps going,
Thinking wakes up and looks for action.
The four seasons make flowers,
Their perfume makes a lamp.
The news hits Ghana and everybody's heart,
The hearts beats well,
They take care of the neighborhood.

Greece

You missed Sir Lover,
That makes the history book.
The book announces today and grabs tomorrow,
Tomorrow cannot do anything,
All the tomorrows line up for the book.
The Greek flag is flown in every country,
Love and compassion appear,
They hang onto the sound of the bell.

Grenada

The pen draws one line
      and a beautiful painting appears.
The painting calls the mountain and sky
      and teaches them.
You throw desire away,
Thinking is clear.
In front of thinking, the mirror cannot move.
You find a friend,
That friend is the mountain and sky.
The mountain and sky show life and death clearly.
All of nature learns from the mountain and sky.

Guatemala

The mind does not make desire.
The mind makes clear thinking.
When you were born, you were perfect,
Your body, thinking, and mind
      come through your lifetime clearly,
      without misfortune.
Each word is very important,
Never throw any away,
The mountain and river converse with you.

Guinea

In the mind, the memory box collects the thoughts.
The thoughts look for the original mirror.
The mirror goes straight to the end point.
The biggest flower makes beauty and clarity.
Its perfume announces Guinea's original face.

Guinea-Bissau

Time makes flowers appear and disappear,
The fruit shines.
How can you understand that point?
The truth's breath hits the sky,
The rich earth creates life and shows greatness,
You never hide the story,
Thinking moves action,
Your thoughts are saintly.

Guyana

The train runs on its tracks,
History is breathing.
That action is beautiful,
The country shines,
Guyana draws the greatest picture.

Haiti

The movement of a good quality life
    is just like swimming,
Nobody can argue about that point.
Understanding each other makes great energy.
That keeps everything clear, no dust appears.
The flowers open and dance,
The flowers dance like the rhythm of chit-chat.

Honduras

The lovers go around the reservoir,
They sit and talk about love,
Their speech is clear,
      just like the reservoir's water.
Their true mind appears,
Lying cannot come near.
The lovers call the mountains and rivers,
With great strength, the mountains and rivers
      show what truth is.
The West and the Sunset
      have an appointment tomorrow.

Hungary

Everyone's face appears on the waving flag,
Their eyes are very shiny.
Each house makes enjoyment and happiness,
They make truth,
They make a country.
The country moves just like a flowing river.

Iceland

Iceland's children are intelligent and sharp.
They open tomorrow brightly.
They work hard, just like a shiny mirror,
The mirror is just like a sword's blade.
The landlords' dreaming makes the cities
      grow bigger.
Iceland stands up stronger,
Its face is so great.

India

People respect each other.
They make a flag and put it on the ground
      and in the sky.
The flag waves.
New faces appear on the flag,
They talk with the sky and earth.
Whoever knows this story,
      writes history correctly and clearly.

Indonesia

People walk on the sidewalk,
Their thoughts become flowers,
Their action is impeccable.
The water moves clearly,
Everything is washed out.
You are always correct and clear,
Nobody complains about that.
Suddenly you get enlightenment,
That is Indonesia's treasure.

Iran

People talk about how to make their country
        correct and clear,
That makes everybody happy.
The trees' leaves learn from the four seasons.
They proclaim their knowledge
        to the rivers and mountains.
The rivers and mountains are silent,
They create new growth every season,
The new flies into the air.

Iraq

Life meets the mirror.
The mirror is silent,
    Its eyes are shiny.
The mirror's eyes' bright enjoyment
    plants each grain of sand.
The children grow up,
In their hearts,
    the biggest flower is dancing.

Ireland

The stars talk with each other in the blue sky,
The flowers talk with each other in the garden,
Someone understands
        that these conversations are the same.
The flowers' perfume carries the country.
You want to go, you arrive at that point.
You work hard, the fortune is waiting for you.
Everybody visits each other,
They talk about the truth of life in the world.
Your foundation makes truth,
The truth helps the ocean become bigger.

Israel

Everybody works hard,
Everybody earns great things.
The wind passes by;
Inside the wind, the seeds' eyes are open.
Tomorrow and the day after tomorrow
      make the four seasons.
You try to understand the truth,
The truth hangs on,
      in the air.

Italy

Wisdom appears and creates Art;
Art creates a great drawing.
Space opens,
Your thoughts are sown across the air.
New history is created,
      it collects energy.
That energy collects sound
      and cuts through the road.
The road is beautiful,
The beauty hangs onto everybody.

Jamaica

The children grow up,
Their hands create great things.
Sounds flow and cut through
    thinking and the mind.
You made everything,
These things never rest today and tomorrow.
Your voice is very clear,
Jamaica is reborn.

Japan

Thinking measures, measures,
    and measures again.
The mind flies in the sky.
The pen point draws,
The calculator fills the air.
The blue ocean's strong waves work hard,
They swallow the blue sky.

Jordan

Your belt is tight,
You never stop working,
That makes the day and night open their eyes.
Strong dirt and strong sky create everything,
They show what is correct
        and what is not correct.

Kazakhstan

Kazakhstan stands up on its own
      Due to the minds of its people.
Everybody controls themselves.
That wisdom creates a greater life,
      everywhere.
Everyone becomes one family.
The artist appears,
The artist likes smooth action.
The road is strong,
The cars line up and drive,
The cars hit the seasons.

Kenya

In the canister, the secret holds on.
Somebody understands what it is about
      and they kiss the canister.
Love and compassion appear.
The Kenyans' hearts hold onto their future dream,
Each dream grows,
The dreams talk with the sky and earth.

Kiribati

The grain grows up.
The mind and thinking shine,
Action cannot argue about that,
Action makes philosophy appear.
Outside and inside are made clear.
No one can argue about that point.
Inside, the fried potato shows what life is,
Wisdom shines brilliantly.

Kuwait

The fork holds onto a great thing,
It looks for its owner,
That makes beauty.
The beautiful makes yes and no, clear.
Not just anybody can do that.
Your résumé appears on your face,
    shining clearly.
The East opens the sky,
The message of the sky's meaning
    goes everywhere.

Kyrgyzstan

The kilogram
>announces what mathematics is,
>everywhere.

$1 + 1 = 2$

The memories are beautiful.
The beautiful enjoy making the past, present
>and future.

That which is 100% perfect
>looks for its owner.

Every tent makes a lamp.
The lamps are bright,
They make the night's beauty the highest.

Lao People's Democratic Republic

The radio broadcast has information for everybody.
People come and go and meet each other,
They create love and compassion.
All kinds of flowers make the rivers
      and mountains shine.
The butterflies and bees are introduced
      to the neighborhood.
The children go to school and enjoy studying.
The children's hearts come together,
That energy makes the country grow.
The compass' eyes open the road,
All life lines up.
Fortunes fill the bowl and dance,
Every neighborhood enjoys that point.
The light goes everywhere,
That energy opens the sky.
The correct brakes know what is clear
      and what is not clear.
Every curve on the road holds a sign,
The signs show the directions.
Everyone's thinking keeps the mind clear.

Latvia

Latvia, your face is shiny.
Your face appears on the ground
 and in the sky.
In your country,
 everyone makes love and compassion.
Everyone shares their energy with each other.
That is the pride of Latvia.

Lebanon

The train tracks go straight for 10,000,000 years.
At the end point, you look at the rivers
      and mountains,
They are clear, like the blue sky.
The birds walk and fly,
They never count the day and night,
That is the wisdom of the birds.
The bird's wisdom
      and the compassion of the people
      are in the same neighborhood.

Lesotho

The clear lesson makes thinking and the mind
        clear like a mirror.
The sky and earth carry their own dreams,
They visit inside when you sleep.
Moment by moment
        you love your neighborhood clearly.
That is the country's happiness.

Liberia

In the noodles, truth takes care of life.
The flower garden is in front of the porch.
The flowers make friends, they love each other.
The clear perfume creates the sky and earth.
Nobody can imitate that.

Libyan Arab Jamahiriya

It is comfortable in the limousine.
Great success opens the road,
The road has no gate.
Your important position makes your success shine.
Breakfast, lunch and dinner show the daily date.

Liechtenstein

The biggest mind has no questions.
That mind looks at the strong mountain,
The mountain's face looks like a star.
Time chases the mountain,
Time never rests.
The original face of the people
 is the original root of the Universe.

Lithuania

You are always polite to guests.
You keep a clear consciousness and a clear mind,
You never change.
You keep going straight.
Everybody has a strong face;
In their lives, people dream,
That creates wealth for their country.
That teaches the next generation,
They make greatness appear.

Luxembourg

You always help,
That is the treasure of the sky and earth.
The hearts of your people never count;
Their hearts show love and compassion.
Sir Sun and Sir Moon visit every single person.
All kinds of fragrances line up and visit the people.

Madagascar

The mind makes a flower.
The mind visits the mountain,
On the mountain's highest point,
    life is breathing.
The families' hands help the neighborhood.
Action is smooth, beauty appears.
Your consciousness is just like a sword blade,
It makes the people's lives clear.

Malawi

The consciousness of silence is
 the same as meditation;
That makes thinking clear.
Trees are tied up together and make houses,
The roof carries the blue sky,
At the foundation is a garden bed,
Nature is shown beautifully.

Malaysia

One word gives life to truth again.
The strong lesson makes knowledge.
Knowledge makes seeds,
The seeds count the past, present and future.
People live clearly, they don't miss anything.
That is the highest point.

Maldives

One word makes an enemy,
One word makes a benefactor.
Check inside the mind,
Love and hate reveal themselves to each other.
The wind passes by and learns from that.

Mali

Talking, talking, talking,
The words pick up the sky and earth
        and drop them.
Nobody stops talking.
On the other side of the earth there is also
        talking, talking, talking,
They never stop.
Life begins with talk and ends with talk.
Inside the hearts of the people,
        the words go into the blood vessels
        and make the organs clear.

Malta

You want to try to stop all thinking,
Still thinking appears.
Action follows thinking,
Action never stops.
When you sleep, dreaming appears,
    You meet someone,
    You make a family, a city, a country,
That country follows its own dream,
    continuously,
        for 10,000,000 years.

Marshall Islands

The Marshallese talk,
They never look back.
The great energy of those words
    is from the Marshallese people.
The wind and clouds always move,
They make a wall around the people's lives.
The people share all their difficulties,
They work hard on everything.
There is food inside the cooking pot,
Its taste makes a happy family.
Persevere against any difficulty,
Behind the mountain the dream is alive,
    waiting for you.

Mauritania

Everybody takes care of each other like one family.
Every life has an excuse.
Everybody is born clearly,
Everybody sings a happy song.
Their future dreaming fills their own country.

Mauritius

Each grain of sand has meaning.
Each grain of sand makes a bed;
The sand makes a mountain.
Where the cars go, the wealthy are dancing.
Your shirts look like you work so hard;
All of your leftover work talks about the truth.

Mexico

You hold onto a mug of beer,
Your history is sometimes sad
      and sometimes happy.
The seeds are pregnant with the sky and earth.
In front of your nose,
      the Universe sticks up its hands.

Micronesia

After one sip of water,
    Breathing is good.
Early in the morning you go to work.
On the way your dream is big.
The tallest mountain carries its own dream
    on its top.
On every road, the guests come and go,
    They enjoy.
You never argue about what is yours
    or what is mine,
That is beautiful.
Your jacket dances and flies into the sky.

Monaco

Your palms look at each other.
They come together and help the neighborhood.
Your hands understand your country.
Life is born and dies,
In life, the great truth opens its eyes.
The scent touches your nose,
That smell is the greatest in the sky and earth.

Mongolia

Flowers are everywhere on our planet.
The flowers pass through the four seasons.
Archeologists run into your heart,
They enjoy what they find there.
Your face appears from your résumé,
Your face can tell the true meaning,
You throw away all sadness and suffering,
You have no gate.

Morocco

Your face doesn't argue,
That is great.
Everyone is beautiful,
You want to help your country,
The road never ends.
The taste of mint gives long life
      to your country's history.

Mozambique

The parents love the highest truth.
The ocean is quiet,
The ocean water is blue.
The ocean water meets the blue sky,
They check each other's face.
Between the ocean and the sky,
The blue mirror holds onto the measure;
The measure puts the blue sky and the ocean
      onto the scale.
The biggest city's face draws
      the history of its people,
The drawing makes no mistake.

Myanmar

Talking is beautiful;
The ears listen and enjoy.
The heart makes happiness.
The industrial machines work hard
        and create energy,
They continue everyday,
That energy goes throughout the world.
The clothes are washed very clearly,
They wait for their owner.

Namibia

Life is born and dies,
Where does it come from?
Where does it go?
Everybody leaves their own shining history,
Don't be attached to anything,
The mirror cannot argue about that.
Thinking digs into the mind,
The mind becomes a mirror.
Your life never misses anything,
That makes the next generation happy.

Nauru

Your river bed is silent.
The earth can understand,
The sky can understand,
The four seasons don't make any mistakes.

Nepal

At the crossroads,
    the silent lamppost shows the way.
Day and night never rest.
The heart beats;
It introduces day and night.
8 x 8 = 64
Nobody can argue about that point,
For their lifetime,
    they bow to the pen and brush.

Netherlands

Tomorrow lines up and helps today.
Today never closes its door,
Today opens wisdom.
The flowers open on the plain,
The flowers understand what today means.
The perfume answers to today.
Laundering makes everything clear,
That clarity is the original face.
You show what true love is,
The baby shouts,
The air shakes.

New Zealand

The news goes out everywhere,
That makes the whole world one family.
You get what you want, or,
      you don't get what you want,
No shadow is left behind.
The teacher tells the students what to do,
The students' eyes and ears open clearly.
You pay your rent on time,
That opens the road to success.
You make your life go well,
That makes New Zealand's face bright.

Nicaragua

You and your friend make a wall
    around Nicaragua's families.
Your voice is so clear,
You talk with your friend.
Every day your face looks great.
Your direction is strong, go straight.
You open every new day.

Niger

In Niger, the love and compassion of its people
        help each other.
All of nature understands that is the original face.
All of nature learns from that.
The faces of the rivers and mountains
        never change,
They always show the color blue.
The blue sky tries to copy that,
The blue sky keeps one position,
It cannot move from that point.

Nigeria

Your résumé follows your years.
The color of every résumé is different,
The résumé's memory keeps itself clear.
Your thinking is very sharp,
The résumé cannot argue.
The résumé carries a person's life.
Early in the morning your mind makes a decision,
You go through the day,
In the nighttime, your mind opens,
Thinking comes out of your mind,
Your thinking makes the night go silent.

Norway

You work hard,
The scale understands that,
The scale never lies.
The scale announces how clear you are
 to the whole world, the sky, and the earth.
The mind learns something,
That makes the mirror clear.
Thinking lines up correctly,
The wedding gown is beautiful,
Just like the sound of the love bell.
Thinking can understand every point,
That is freedom,
It fills in, everywhere.

Oman

The road is open.
People come and go,
The road never holds a gate.
In the four seasons,
Each season hosts the next,
That makes them free.
The mind has a good feeling,
Thinking creates a flower,
Action creates perfume,
That is the highest point of truth.

Pakistan

The sound of the wind oscillates;
The wind carries all the news,
It tumbles and tumbles.
Where the wind goes, it cuts through ears.
The wind makes the eyes bright,
The wind makes everything grow.
The beginning and ending of everything
    are measured.
Tomorrow, Sir Sun has an appointment
    with the western sky,
The strong road welcomes everyone
    and everything.

Palau

Your heart beats strongly,
That is the foundation of healthy roots.
The perfume opens its mouth and says
      that the hearts of the flowers in the garden
      beat strongly, day by day.
The compass shows East, West, South and North,
      the points never end,
The compass announces what great freedom is.
Everybody claps their hands,
The sound is like thunder,
That makes Palau happy.

Panama

Each scallion announces the news of the ground.
The ground's energy introduces how great life is.
Inside Panama, all villages are connected
      with bridges.
Love and happiness continue,
They respect that life is very important.

Papua New Guinea

Dig into the ground.
Inside, the seeds open their mouths,
Their faces appear, green.
The seeds' faces shoot out onto the ground
        and make everybody happy.
All the news is announced everywhere.
The news hits the heart.
The heart becomes a mirror that makes dreaming.
You are never lazy,
Your body's action is a treasure to the world,
No one can copy that,
Only a Saint can understand it.

Paraguay

The blue eyes read what love is.
The mirror runs and returns the rain barrel;
Everybody's face is there, inside.
When the birds fly, they never drop their dreams.
Inside the biggest forest, all forms of life
      live together,
The mountains make a screen around the forest,
The mountains open their green eyes,
This mountain and that mountain make everything
        into one family.

Peru

The sound goes out,
It shakes the river and mountain.
The river and mountain listen from inside,
Their ears never lie.
The wind passes by,
The wind tries to open its ears,
The wind runs to the clouds.
On the mountain, a house is built.
The house checks the past, present and future,
Inside your mind, the sky and earth
      play and enjoy.

Philippines

The clouds, rain, stream, and river water
　　　always appear when necessary,
They are never thirsty.
The bell never makes an excuse,
It knows when the time comes, to ring.
The flower bud is thirsty for Spring.
The power of support makes everybody
　　　able to enjoy.

Poland

Your name is Poland.
If anybody hears your name,
 they never forget it.
The morning Sun and nighttime Moon
 understand your name,
They visit you.
The Sun and Moon give beauty to everybody.
Everybody can understand that,
Their faces are filled with joy.

Portugal

Portugal, your energy is great.
If everyone wants something,
You don't build walls between.
You dance,
You smile,
You enjoy,
You make happiness.
Everybody has the job of helping each other,
Everybody picks up the shiny day.

Qatar

In the ground, the dirt makes a box for each seed.
The seeds make life.
They shoot out over the ground.
The seeds get great energy from the sky and earth.
They collect air and water,
The seeds open their own dreaming,
Their dreams cover the mountain and river,
       beautifully.
Even when the seeds are at their lowest energy,
       they don't give up.
That is Qatar's great treasure.

South Korea

The lamp is in front of your nose.
Inside the light, the universe is dancing.
Your consciousness is very strong,
It hits the earth and cuts through the sky.
You understand or you don't understand,
It doesn't matter,
Your country's name is famous,
The name is Sham Chun Lee Gum Su Gang San.

'Sham Chun Lee' means: 1200 Kilometers
'Gum Su Gang San' means: Gold Land and Mountains

Republic of Moldova

Your great consciousness makes clear thinking.
It opens the front and the back, clearly.
Life arrives in Moldova,
Breathing in and breathing out
	shakes the rivers and mountains.
The people's faces and hands help each other
	for their lifetime,
Their hearts beat strongly.

Romania

Rowing helps the boat cut through
      the river and ocean.
If anybody wants something,
The boat makes a road for them.
Everyday, the day is bright,
That makes you and I understand.
The brightness visits every house,
It takes care of everything,
That is great.
If somebody doesn't know Romania,
Romania can introduce them.

Russian Federation

People visit Russia and study it.
Their knowledge makes a new book.
The book doesn't talk,
Anyone can read the book.
The grass and trees cut through time and space,
They make one family,
They never argue.
The grass and trees invite everybody
      and teach the highest knowledge,
The air watches them.

Rwanda

The people who live in Rwanda study the truth.
Sir Sun arrives,
The Rwandans introduce the truth to Sir Sun.
Sir Sun leaves and the Stars try to understand,
Their ears are bright.
People are compassionate to each other,
They talk about what truth is continuously
      for 10,000,000 years.

Saint Kitts and Nevis

Two pieces give to each other, that is compassion.
Love is necessary in people's society.
The truck never stops showing its own life.
Memories of the past have their own meaning.
Minds can understand each other.
One who has difficulty working is helped.
Your strong energy makes your future dreams
      bigger,
The measure can understand your mind.
The loom dances happily while it weaves the fabric,
The golf ball cuts through the air,
The ball knows where it will land.

Saint Lucia

You can understand people's lives,
You can also understand the mountain and the sky.
People's energy, knowledge and wisdom are from
        the root of the Universe.
Your mind opens,
You are compassionate to your neighborhood,
You talk to each other,
The piece of white paper enjoys that.
Time understands the minutes,
The minutes understand the seconds,
They all take care of each other.
You never exhibit your own ego,
That is wisdom,
That is Saint Lucia's treasure.

Saint Vincent and the Grenadines

All the world's people are great.
Everybody introduces each other to the blue sky.
Life is a sensation.
They don't pick on each other,
They enjoy their life.
They know how to count, add, and subtract.
From the top of the highest mountain,
The perfume fills your country.
Everyone's mind becomes one,
Your people are born by human beings,
They never brag about themselves,
Their hearts are grand.

Samoa

If you cut through your own desire,
You can taste the truth.
You wake up your love and compassion,
When your people come together,
      they understand each other,
They help each other;
The grass and trees also learn from you.
You make clear what suffering is
      and what enjoyment is.
That technique is the greatest in the sky and earth.

San Marino

Everything is in the bag of rice.
Your thinking looks for its chance in the rice bag.
Every village works hard,
They make the laziest wake up.
You make your own desire.
So many difficulties are in front of you,
You work hard.
Everything becomes free,
Freedom makes your people take care
    of each other,
That point is the beginning of life.

Sao Tome and Principe

Ice cannot control the temperature.
The farm makes flowers,
The flowers' rhythm enjoys itself, beautifully.
The four seasons appear all together,
They make each individual season,
They never threaten each other,
    They always love each other.
The seeds make history greater,
The mudslide causes new to be created,
Everybody gets their fortune.

Saudi Arabia

In the mind, the highest is love.
Your thoughts look for their foundation.
The sand tries to explain what the foundation is.
The wind passes by, without comment.
The great sunlight fills the day.
The desert is empty,
The desert holds the biggest house.
Nobody knows the biggest house's secret,
In the house, a different kind of life dances.

Senegal

Senegal counts the numbers.
The numbers line up,
They are busy all day long.
The day determines the jobs,
History follows them.
You train, you study, you learn.
Through your concentration,
Your country grows up again.

Serbia and Montenegro

The last words are spoken,
The dirt listens.
After, the dirt washes its ears, again.
The dirt looks to the sky,
In the sky, the stars are so quiet,
Their eyes are so shiny.
The stars' light plants the dew,
The dew makes steam fly,
It make the morning open,
Buddha points to the empty mind,
Somebody understands that point,
Their mind becomes like that of a child.

Seychelles

Each lifetime makes its own history,
That makes everything wake up.
Your mind always goes straight,
The worker is successful from not being lazy.
Sir Sun always goes West,
East is already pregnant with Sir Sun.

Sierra Leone

The heart of every seed carries the sky and earth.
The seeds open,
      Their new faces appear.
The seeds' eyes open and see the birds flying back.
The cloud wants to visit,
The cloud counts is footsteps,
It looks for Sir Lover,
All the seeds smile.

Singapore

The fresh vegetables hold their own dreams.
They look for people,
They draw the people's faces.
Every house fills with love and compassion.
The fireworks make the country bright, everywhere.

Slovakia

Everybody's face shines with their own stories,
They hold their slogans up in the air.
The cars line up on the road everywhere.
The minds of the people fill the road.
The car tires work hard,
they never brag about themselves.
The day passes smoothly,
The successful way keeps going straight.
Someone understands that,
Their eyes shine,
That makes Slovakia bright.

Slovenia

Slowly, the sunlight appears;
It carries the sky and earth,
It keeps going straight, all day long.
The day never stops.
The mind becomes clear,
Thinking is sharp,
Spring runs in and arrives.
Spring makes flowers on the mountains and rivers.
The beautiful song is enjoyed,
The wind copies the song.
Your work is not done,
That makes tomorrow's eyes open.

Solomon Islands

You try to live,
You work hard,
Good fortune runs to you.
Throughout your life,
      you take good care of your health,
You tell breakfast, lunch and dinner your secret.
You can drive, you can go anywhere.
Early in the morning, the flowers open,
The early riser meets the flowers.
The lens can pick out the truth.
You complete a difficult undertaking,
Your face is beautiful,
You attain everything.

Somalia

The young girl herds the cows,
Her heart creates a mind flower.
The horses understand the young girl's mind,
They all run in.
The girl, the cows, and the horses bring prosperity
      to the mountains and the plains;
That action is the same as the compassion
      of a mother and father.
That is proclaimed all over the world.

South Africa

The day is so hot, just like a sauna.
The Sun looks for a place to rest,
It invites the clouds.
The clouds make thunder and lightning,
The lightning makes the sky and earth bright.
The grass and trees appear by themselves,
The rain carries no pain,
The rain water goes everywhere
      in the streams and rivers,
The streams and rivers understand
      how to go to the ocean.
The ocean's strong waves look at South Africa.

Spain

Karma comes and goes,
It makes people's lives thicker and thinner.
The painter creates a beautiful picture,
The paint gives every house new clothes,
The paint insists on being bound
      with the people's history.

Sri Lanka

You triumph over your awful suffering.
The heaven of good fortune is waiting for you.
After cutting through their own desire,
Everybody is so beautiful.
The flower grows up itself, beautifully,
The perfume never brags about itself.
Sri Lanka's mind is clear, like a well.
Everybody says, "That is magnificent!"

Sudan

The trees and grass line up and teach each other.
The sky and earth cut through the four seasons,
The sky and earth learn from the grass and trees.
After gaining knowledge, the dirt does very well.
The sky is stronger than before,
Its blue color appears deeper than before.
From their lifetimes of training and studying,
The Sudanese attain their own philosophy.
That is great,
That creates a new world.

Suriname

Everybody tries to make the beginning and end
    the same.
They make their dreams clear,
They collect all the dreams
    and put them in the four seasons.
The mountains and rivers understand that point,
The mountains' and rivers' answer makes
    the flowers open.
Everybody makes friends,
Their lives are clear,
They continue and never end.

Swaziland

In the water, the fish exhibit their dancing,
That is the ocean's art.
That art teaches people.
Inside the people's hearts,
    Their minds make a flower.
On the face of the earth,
    All this is true,
    All this is great,
    All this is beautiful.
You can understand this point.
Everybody opens their chests,
Thinking is busy,
All day it looks for something to do.

Sweden

The many mountains never brag to each other,
The white snow is clear.
It talks with the blue sky about what is true.
The highest point and the lowest point
      are divided clearly,
That makes everybody happy.
Dancing makes the highest happiness,
The heart beating in the chest understands
      what is secret.
The secret of health shakes the people's minds.

Switzerland

The corn grows strongly in the cornfield,
That makes the mountain wealthy.
The corn is pregnant with the Swiss' love.
People respect their elders,
The mind shows a clear mirror.
In the evening, the flower opens,
The flower is never scared of the night.
The rental car has so many different owners,
Their faces appear,
Their memories talk about what is right now.

Syrian Arab Republic

The mountains, rivers, grass, and trees
    wash themselves.
The cloud dances,
It hides in the rain.
The grass and trees understand the rain,
They make the streams.
The streams' and rivers' water
    are never jealous of each other,
That shocks the ocean.
Sir Sun carries the news and runs into Syria.
The Syrian morning wakes up.

Tajikistan

Compassion appears like strong fire.
Compassion invites love,
      they are introduced to each other.
You want something very strongly,
Heaven can feel that.
If you want something, only go straight.
You make your own dream bigger,
In your dream, you can understand who you are.
That makes a strong road.

Thailand

It is your custom to always respect guests,
All the world's people learn from that.
The airplane flies up,
What kind of dreams do its passengers have?
The airplane lands down on the ground,
People realize that the ground is so graceful.
Your action is not added to or subtracted from,
That is your original root.

The former Yugoslav Republic of Macedonia

You appear in your mind,
You can see who you are.
Thinking circles around,
Your face and my face make a new face.
Everybody wants to dream,
They don't want to miss anything
         in their lifetime.

Timor-Leste

The Universe cannot move.
The Universe doesn't know what to do
      about the secret inside the splinter.
The mind carries everything,
It keeps going, continuously.
Thinking and the body learn from the mind.
After being born,
Everybody studies themselves,
It is their homework,
      For their lifetime.

Togo

The growing grain shows
      how well the people tend the earth.
The compassion of the people is equal,
All of nature learns about that.
The water says it is water,
The air says it is air,
The dirt says it is dirt,
The sky says it is the sky,
The truth is dancing.

Tonga

The mind doesn't make excuses,
Thinking is great,
Action shows the philosophy.
The family has its own rules,
The families help each other.
One flower sees what they do,
That flower has great meaning,
It is sown into its perfume.

Trinidad and Tobago

The characters in fiction hide their own secrets.
People on the other side of the world
    don't understand these secrets,
They come running straight in.
The pen point flies everywhere
    on each page of the book,
The stories are great.
Where do the stories come from,
    where do the stories go?
Sir Moon delivers the dreams for the stories.
The lovers enjoy each other,
That makes the eyes of the new generation open.
The cooking pot understands something,
The cooking pot shouts to the sky.
Every Saturday the music plays,
The music invites all the neighborhood.
All the people share their compassion equally,
That is the treasure of Trinidad and Tobago.

Tunisia

You completely stop all your thinking,
Then you cannot open your mouth.
The truth can make one flower open.
You understand truth and love and compassion,
That is our planet's heaven.
If you look down on others,
You cannot understand who you are.
Every morning you wash your own face,
The day tells you that you are great.

Turkey

In every house the dust and dirt are cleaned,
That makes the homes clean and bright.
The parents make their daughters and sons grow,
That is the real flower,
The parents always enjoy that.
The country claps its hands and shakes the sky,
The ground also dances.

Turkmenistan

The loom weaves fabric.
The Turkmen love that fabric.
The children grow up,
Their minds are so clear,
That makes their future prosperous.
The truth teaches you
      what the Messiah's message is about.
The descending road returns back,
The way opens again.
The sharp blade slices between good and bad,
The flower knows how to spread its seeds
      on the rich earth.

Tuvalu

You keep strength and weakness,
That makes life appear in 10,000 different ways.
The successful understand truth.
The country needs them,
That is the city society's roots.
The city's expanded dream makes the country strong.
You always talk about good and bad,
      point by point,
The future generation makes a flower,
That is the new life's strong face.

Uganda

The grass and trees don't have an umbrella,
They are never shy,
They make the mountain's strong face.
The birds sing and brag about themselves,
That makes the mountain happy.
Sometimes thunder and lightening appear,
And everybody wakes up.
Every year is so busy,
You miss something, also you have happiness;
They come and go.
Sir Sun makes a big announcement to everybody;
Sir Sun makes the sky blue and the ground green.

Ukraine

The weeping willow branches move softly,
The wind announces Spring,
The wind invites the clouds,
The clouds makes the hills and mountains wealthy.
Tomorrow and after tomorrow,
      their faces stay the same.
The day and night make deep history.
You can digest the difficulties,
That renews the lives of the people.

United Arab Emirates

You look at our planet very carefully,
Each time, it gets older.
Our planet and its people think the same thought
    at the same time,
Our planet never argues,
It keeps clear.
Hot and cold water understand the cloud,
The rule can make the highest and lowest point
    clear,
Lead understands metal.
You are confused,
The mirror shows you what is clear.
You cut through attachment and desire,
The sand opens its chest for you.
The lesson of the highest point
    can understand the original face,
The beginning can understand how to end.

United Kingdom of Great Britain and Northern Ireland

The splinters understand how to show themselves.
The grain is the kingdom,
All kinds of insects run in to the grain,
The grain feeds them.
The truth always opens its eyes,
      Season by season, continuously.
The rag understands how to clean the dirt, clearly.
You want something,
A lesson always follows behind.
You make great works,
You cut all thinking,
Your thoughts are clear and shiny.
You make a decision,
Nobody can argue about it.
The ocean makes strong waves,
The color of the waves appear clearly.
People come and go,
The ocean entertains them.
There is a big shock in the news,
People grab that news,
They look for their own consciousness.
The children are all clear,
How did they get that way?
Your mind hits the mirror.
The seeds land on the ground,
The flower opens,
It exhibits itself to the sky and earth.

United Republic of Tanzania

The sidewalk opens the big road,
The road has no gate.
You understand who you are.
Your action controls the day - day in and day out.
You never call yourself.
Your energy keeps going straight forward.
The strongest energy picks up the earth and sky,
And drops them.

United States of America

The nightclub is fashionable,
The ideas of fashion and your thoughts are the same,
    They open the road.
Somebody argues, someone else makes them stop,
That someone knows subtraction
    and addition clearly.
Technology controls itself well,
That sensation creates wealth.
Each time the news blows out,
All the world's people try to open their ears
    and listen.
The mind comes and goes,
It fixes the bad habit.
You are called the morning country,
All the world's people come to you,
The melody of the ocean waves is clear,
Your mind tries to understand the minds of the
    parents and teachers.
The nightclub's strobe light dreams
    about tomorrow,
The strobe counts on Sir Moon's dreaming.
The road is made bigger,
The road waits for everybody.

Uruguay

Style is beautiful,
That makes our planet Earth enjoy its tumbling.
During rush hour,
    There are so many cars,
    Everyone is shocked,
    Their consciousness wakes up.
The Uruguayans' coming and going never stops.
Every road's eye light is so warm.
You always tell the truth, clearly,
Heaven wants that way.

Uzbekistan

Look at the mountain,
The other side of the mountain
      dreams about this side.
That great dream is put into the wind,
The wind carries that dream and runs into the book,
Inside, the book talks about the truth.
The mind can understand what is true.
Thinking makes seeds and spreads them out.
The face of the city is so crowded,
It counts on the minds of its people.
Thinking gets life from the big and small things.
The wind passes by, pinches everything,
      and makes everything breathe.
The strong cloud makes the sky and earth
      be reborn again.

Vanuatu

After the grass is cut, it shows new life beginning,
The grass shows what quality life means.
Someone understands the truth,
They announce that truth never changes.
Fire is always hot, ice is always cold.
Someone understands that that truth
      opens in front of your country,
That is the flower of hope.
You want freedom, you work hard;
You try hard to control yourself;
That makes the angels look for you.

Venezuela

The pillow understands dreaming,
The warm blanket also understands.
You dreamt,
      the dream reads the day.
The highest studying can understand the mind,
The blackboard's eyes never forget
      how the white chalk makes up its face.
The blackboard thinks it owns the knowledge,
It makes itself bigger,
The future dreams run onto the blackboard,
      and shows what thinking is
      and what mind is.
You understand who you are,
Also you can understand your family.
Love begins there,
You can taste the truth.

Viet Nam

Inside, the organs never rest,
They work hard 24 hours a day.
Everybody learns from their organs.
The ocean also never rests, it only works hard.
The paddy field makes the rice perfectly,
Each stalk knows when to bow.
People come and go, North and South,
There are no gates,
The mountain river enjoys that.

Yemen

The wisdom of the people is how to live,
    past and present.
The mountain says it can understand that,
The water says it can understand that.
The first person to hear the mountain and the water
    opens his ears;
He looks to the blue sky,
Heaven's angels are there;
The movement of the angels makes the stars shine.
The stars' light is clear,
It shines on Yemen's face;
The light shines for thousands
    and thousands of year.

Zambia

The children sleep,
Their faces make clear dreaming.
Their dreams carry the sky and earth,
    and tumble.
After it rains, the ground is so strong.
The walking feet enjoy that.
The mind can understand Zambia,
The mind makes thinking wake up.

Zimbabwe

The lock creates belief,
The lock has no eyes,
The lock has a strong chest,
The lock can open and close all of nature,
That is the lock's freedom.
You want something,
Your two palms pray,
In your palms, your heart beats clearly.
You pass through many difficulties and suffering,
You become successful,
The perfume announces your great successful face.
The ocean water carries everything,
The earth understands it has grown up,
The ocean waves' white foam smiles.

The Universe

The Universe's chest carries all the stars,
Nobody knows its exact size.
The telescope open its eyes,
It tries to measure the Universe's chest.
The telescope needs human knowledge,
It knocks on the heads of the people.
The Universe lays its body down.
All the stars come together and sit,
They talk about their dreams,
Their dreams fill the Universe's body.
The Universe's body has no clothes,
People's eyes try to understand the Universe,
But they cannot measure its body.
The Universe jumps into the minds of the people,
Still, their minds are empty.
The Universe understands that the mind is bigger
    than itself.
The Universe looks for a measure.
The measure says that it can measure the Universe,
But it cannot measure the human mind.
The Universe picks up the measure
    and takes it to the scale,
The scale has no comment.
The Universe is so frustrated.
The tape measure cannot measure
    the Universe's speed.
The moment grabs the Universe,
The moment picks up a second and hangs it
    on the Universe.
The second measures the Universe's speed,
In one second, the Universe moves
    30,000,000 miles,

The Universe's energy is so strong,
      nobody can handle it.
One small piece of dust wants to wrestle,
The Universe and the dust wrestle,
Finally the Universe's face and body turn into dust.
The dust smiles,
It has nowhere to go.

The Stars

The Stars appear by themselves.
Each Star's dream shines.
That is the Stars' heaven.
The Stars always tell the truth,
They never lie to each other,
The Stars mirror each other,
The Stars know how to be close to each other,
They use their own shadow,
That is their wisdom.
Each Star has life,
Their lives come and go,
Their lives breathe in and out.
The human mind checks every Star,
Every Star jumps into the human mind,
The human mind is still empty,
The Stars don't understand why,
They question each other.
The mirror moves softly close to the Stars,
The Stars finally understand emptiness.

Earth

The Earth holds the ocean water,
The ocean water makes friends
    with the land and the islands.
Each life appears,
Each life brings its own dream.
The ocean water makes their dreams grow up.
People use everything on this planet,
The ocean water washes out everything
    that is left over
    and returns it to its original state.
The ocean water wants to become brothers
    with the air.
It asks the air for the beginning and end
    of the news,
The ocean foam dreams, continuously.

The United Nations

Everybody tries to communicate,
Each individual makes a drawing inside their heart,
    And everyone becomes friends.
Each country introduces what they
    are renowned for,
All countries become neighbors,
That is beautiful.
Sometimes, some countries argue,
Nobody likes that.
As the United Nations gets older,
    greater difficulties come through.
This world is in a state of confusion.
Each country looks to themselves,
Everybody concentrates clearly,
    Makes Peace,
    And makes one family.
The United Nations' direction is made clear,
    and then clear thinking points
    inside everyone's mind.
The mind has no color,
Everybody understands,
All their minds become one.
The Stars announce that the United Nations' name
    comes from the root of the Universe.
Our planet understands that,
Our planet circles and circles and draws,
That is emptiness,
Just like the mind.
Our planet always circles and circles
    and tumbles and tumbles,
It never complains about itself.

The Countries of the United Nations

About Zen Master Chang Sik Kim

Zen Master Chang Sik Kim was born in 1944 in the small farming village Go Hak Ri Cun Mal, Gu Chang Goon Ma Ri Myun in Gyung Nam State, South Korea. His formal academic education consisted of three years of elementary school. When he was 13, he entered the Hwa Gye Sa Zen Temple in Seoul and studied under Zen Master Seung Sahn Lee. When Zen Master Kim was 21, he went on a 100 day retreat. During this retreat, martial art forms were revealed to Zen Master Kim through his meditation. During his retreat, Zen Master Kim had a spiritual awakening and attained enlightenment becoming the 79th Patriarch of his Dharma lineage. Zen Master Kim called his art Shim Gum Do which means Mind Sword Path. The art of Shim Gum Do is comprised of six parts: Sword; Shin Boep (Shin Boep means Body Dharma; it is a weaponless art); Ho Shin Sul (Ho Shin Sul means 'self defense'; it is a system of breaking holds, joint locks and pressure points); Long Stick; Two Sword; and Short Stick. The art of Shim Gum Do brings to life a way that unites the emptiness of Zen with the energy of movement and action. The forms of Shim Gum Do teach martial art techniques and their flow of energy realigning the body's natural energy pathways.

Following completion of his retreat, Zen Master Chang Sik Kim formally introduced Shim Gum Do at his temple during a ceremony. His opening words were: "In this degenerate age the demon is strong and the Dharma is weak. Attached to machine technology, we lose our true self, lose the true way and cannot find true life and true direction of consciousness. This world is full of suffering, complications and fighting amongst us. Soon humanity will disappear by itself. Unable to witness this suffering, we rise up with vigor, establish Shim Gum Do and use the Buddha's Great Vow of Great Love and Great Compassion." Zen Master Kim's life work has been devoted to teaching the Dharma through Shim Gum Do. He has taught in the United States for 30 years and also has established centers in Korea and Italy. His temple, Shim Gwang Sa (The Mind Light Temple), is located in the Brighton neighborhood of Boston, Massachusetts.

Zen Master Kim's Shim Gum Do forms are works of art so it was a natural progression for him to express his insights through other means. In 1989 Zen Master Kim began to write poetry. Since then, he has written more than 11,000 poems. His poems are diverse covering a wide range of subjects and styles. They tell stories. They paint pictures in your mind. They are Zen koans. They describe universal energy and show how real this energy is in our everyday lives; even in simple actions. The poems show humanity as part of nature and they also show the humanity of the natural world. Through their imagery, they illustrate how all things in the universe are interconnected.

Zen Master Kim is a member of the Korean P.E.N. Center and also a member of International P.E.N. Zen Master Kim's previous books are: *The Art of Zen Sword*, *The History of Shim Gum Do* and six poetry books: *The Pillowhead Collects Your Dreams*; *Happy Birthday to You*; *The Sky Is Blue, The Water Is Clear*; The *Stars Shine, The Ocean Is Blue*; *The World's*

Flowers, and *The Wind Never Stops*. Zen Master Kim's poems have also appeared in the French edition of the Korean P.E.N.'s *Korean Literature Today*.

Shim Gum Do Founding Master Zen Master Chang Sik Kim lives and teaches at his temple, Shim Gwang Sa, where programs include daily classes in Shim Gum Do and residential Zen training. For more information about Zen Master Kim's other publications or for information about Shim Gum Do, please contact:

World Shim Gum Do Association
203 Chestnut Hill Avenue
Brighton, Massachusetts 02135
(617) 787-1506
www.shimgumdo.org

Mary Jeanette Stackhouse Kim
Shim Gwang Sa Abbot
World Shim Gum Do Head Master
October, 2003